Mexican Grilling and BBQ 100 Outdoor Recipes

By Morris Binner

Contents

Chapter 1: Salsas and Marinades 8

Chapter 2: Grilled Vegetables 18

Chapter 3: Seafood Specials 27

Chapter 4: Chicken Dishes 36

Chapter 5: Pork Delights 45

Chapter 6: Beef Favorites 54

Chapter 7: Tacos and Tostadas 64

Chapter 8: Burgers and Sandwiches 73

Chapter 9: Sides and Street Foods 81

Chapter 10: Desserts and Drinks 90

Appendices and Tips 98

    Mastering Mexican Grilling and BBQ 98

    Spice Guide for Mexican Grilling 99

    Essential Grilling Techniques 100

    Tips for Perfecting Mexican BBQ 102

Introduction

Mexico's rich culinary heritage is a celebration of flavors, colors, and aromas that come alive, especially when cooked outdoors. From street vendors' sizzling taco grills to family gatherings around a backyard barbecue, Mexican grilling and barbecue traditions are woven into the fabric of Mexican life, bringing people together over shared meals. With techniques that have evolved over centuries and flavors drawn from Mexico's diverse regions, Mexican grilling is as much about community and celebration as it is about delicious food. This book, *Mexican Grilling and BBQ: 100 Outdoor Recipes*, is your guide to recreating the authentic tastes of Mexico on your own grill, no matter where you are.

The Tradition of Mexican Outdoor Cooking

Cooking outdoors has been part of Mexican culture since ancient times, tracing back to indigenous tribes who cooked over open fires, using simple yet effective methods to prepare meals. These methods evolved as Spanish colonization introduced new ingredients and techniques, leading to the blend of flavors that define Mexican cuisine today. Many traditional recipes, from fire-roasted salsas to marinated meats, are rooted in techniques passed down through generations. Grilling outdoors is an extension of these age-old customs, blending rustic preparation methods with modern tastes and showcasing Mexico's unique approach to barbecue.

Across the diverse regions of Mexico, grilling traditions vary significantly. In the north, meat reigns supreme with beef cuts like arrachera (skirt steak) seasoned simply with salt and grilled to perfection, often served with charred green onions and a sprinkle of lime juice. Meanwhile, in the coastal regions, fresh seafood takes center stage, with recipes featuring whole fish grilled with bright, zesty marinades. As we journey through these recipes, you'll see how each region contributes to the rich tapestry of flavors in Mexican grilling, each with its own unique influences and techniques.

Essential Ingredients in Mexican Grilling

Mexican barbecue is defined by its bold flavors, achieved through the use of a variety of herbs, spices, and fresh ingredients. Key components of Mexican grilling include marinades made with ingredients like lime juice, garlic, and cilantro, which tenderize and add depth to meats. Dried and fresh chiles are another cornerstone, providing not only heat but also complexity and smokiness to dishes. From earthy guajillo chiles to fiery habaneros, chiles bring both flavor and a characteristic Mexican spice.

Other indispensable ingredients include cumin, oregano, and coriander, all of which add layers of flavor to marinades, rubs, and sauces. Lime is frequently used to add brightness and balance to these bold flavors, cutting through the richness of meats and bringing harmony to each bite. Mexican grilling also relies heavily on fresh vegetables and herbs; cilantro, green onions, and tomatoes are often found on the grill alongside meats, enhancing the dishes with freshness and texture. Whether preparing a marinade or a salsa, each ingredient in Mexican outdoor cooking plays a role in creating a vibrant and unforgettable meal.

Techniques in Mexican Grilling and BBQ

Mexican grilling embraces a variety of cooking techniques, from slow-smoking to direct grilling over hot coals. One of the most iconic methods is *al pastor*, which involves marinating pork in a mixture of dried chiles, spices, and pineapple, then stacking the marinated meat on a vertical spit to cook. Traditionally, *al pastor* is cooked on a rotisserie, similar to shawarma, a technique influenced by Middle Eastern immigrants. The result is tender, juicy meat with a delicious caramelized exterior, sliced thinly and served in warm tortillas.

Another popular method is *barbacoa*, a slow-cooking process where meats, usually lamb or goat, are wrapped in maguey leaves and cooked in an underground pit. This method infuses the meat with a smoky, earthy flavor, making it tender and flavorful. For a similar experience at home, this book provides adaptations that mimic the slow-cooked results of traditional barbacoa, allowing you to recreate these flavors on a standard grill.

Mexican grilling also includes open-fire roasting for vegetables, such as charring tomatoes, onions, and jalapeños to make *salsas asadas* (roasted salsas). This technique intensifies the natural flavors of vegetables, giving salsas a deep, smoky taste that complements grilled meats beautifully. Direct grilling of steaks, chicken, and seafood is also popular, often using marinades and rubs that are quickly seared over high heat, locking in juices and creating a charred, flavorful crust.

The Social Aspect of Mexican Grilling

One of the most cherished aspects of Mexican grilling is the way it brings people together. In Mexico, a barbecue is more than just a meal; it's a celebration, a reason for family and friends to gather and share stories, laughter, and the joy of good food. Known as an *asado* or *carne asada*, these gatherings are often informal yet filled with tradition, with each person playing a role, from grilling the meat to preparing sides like guacamole, rice, and beans. The sounds of sizzling meat, the warmth of the fire, and the aroma of fresh tortillas on the griddle create an inviting atmosphere that draws everyone in.

Mexican barbecues are typically accompanied by lively music, refreshing drinks, and a variety of small dishes, turning a simple outdoor meal into a memorable event. This book encourages you to embrace the social aspect of grilling and create an environment where everyone feels involved, whether it's preparing marinades, assembling tacos, or simply enjoying each other's company. Grilling, for many Mexicans, is as much about the experience of togetherness as it is about the food itself.

What You'll Find in This Book

Mexican Grilling and BBQ: 100 Outdoor Recipes offers a comprehensive collection of recipes that capture the heart and soul of Mexican outdoor cooking. Organized by categories, you'll find a range of dishes suited for every taste—from classic tacos and grilled seafood to inventive sides and salsas. Each recipe has been adapted for the home cook, ensuring that you can bring the flavors of Mexico's rich grilling culture to your backyard with ease.

Each chapter begins with an overview of traditional ingredients and techniques, guiding you through the preparation process with tips and tricks to enhance your grilling experience. You'll learn how to master essential marinades, perfect your grilling methods, and create complementary sides and salsas that elevate each dish. From novice grillers to seasoned barbecue enthusiasts, there's something for everyone in this book, providing a versatile guide to creating authentic Mexican flavors.

As you explore these recipes, remember that Mexican grilling is all about embracing the moment, sharing food, and making memories. Let this book be your companion as you discover new flavors, techniques, and the joy of gathering around the grill. With *Mexican Grilling and BBQ*, you're not just preparing a meal—you're bringing a piece of Mexico's vibrant culinary heritage into your home.

Chapter 1: Salsas and Marinades

1. Salsa Verde for Grilling

Description:
Salsa Verde is a tangy, slightly spicy sauce made from tomatillos, jalapeños, and fresh cilantro. This salsa adds a burst of flavor to grilled meats, especially chicken or pork, and can be used as a marinade or a topping.

Ingredients:

- 5 tomatillos, husked and rinsed
- 1 jalapeño, stemmed and seeded

- 1/4 cup fresh cilantro, chopped
- Juice of 1 lime
- Salt to taste

Instructions:

1. Grill tomatillos and jalapeño until charred, then allow to cool.
2. Blend with cilantro, lime juice, and salt until smooth.
3. Use as a marinade for meats or as a topping for grilled dishes.

---

2. Smoky Chipotle Marinade

Description:
This Smoky Chipotle Marinade, made with chipotle peppers in adobo, garlic, and lime juice, adds a bold, smoky heat to beef or pork. It's ideal for those who enjoy a robust, spicy flavor.

Ingredients:

- 2 tbsp chipotle peppers in adobo sauce
- 2 cloves garlic, minced
- Juice of 1 lime
- 1/4 cup olive oil
- Salt and pepper to taste

Instructions:

1. In a bowl, mix chipotle peppers, garlic, lime juice, olive oil, salt, and pepper.
2. Use to marinate beef or pork for 2–4 hours before grilling.

3. Grill as desired, basting with any remaining marinade.

---

3. Guajillo Chile Salsa

Description:
Guajillo Chile Salsa has a deep, earthy flavor with mild heat, perfect for grilled meats or tacos. Made with dried guajillo chiles, tomatoes, and garlic, this salsa adds a rich, smoky touch to any dish.

Ingredients:

- 4 dried guajillo chiles, stemmed and seeded
- 2 tomatoes, chopped
- 1 clove garlic, minced
- 1/4 cup water
- Salt to taste

Instructions:

1. Toast guajillo chiles in a skillet until fragrant, then soak in warm water for 15 minutes.
2. Blend chiles, tomatoes, garlic, and water until smooth.
3. Season with salt and serve with grilled meats or tacos.

---

4. Lime-Cilantro Marinade

Description:
Lime-Cilantro Marinade is a bright, fresh mix of lime juice, cilantro, and garlic. This marinade is fantastic for chicken or seafood, adding a citrusy, herbaceous flavor that's perfect for grilling.

Ingredients:

- Juice of 2 limes
- 1/4 cup fresh cilantro, chopped
- 2 cloves garlic, minced
- 2 tbsp olive oil
- Salt and pepper to taste

Instructions:
1. Mix lime juice, cilantro, garlic, olive oil, salt, and pepper in a bowl.
2. Use to marinate chicken or seafood for 1–2 hours before grilling.
3. Grill as desired, garnishing with fresh cilantro.

---

5. Adobo Sauce

Description:
Adobo Sauce is a rich, spicy marinade made from a blend of dried chiles, vinegar, and spices. This versatile sauce adds depth to pork and chicken, offering a smoky, slightly tangy taste.

Ingredients:
- 4 dried ancho chiles, stemmed and seeded
- 1/4 cup white vinegar
- 2 cloves garlic, minced
- 1 tsp ground cumin
- Salt and pepper to taste

Instructions:

1. Soak ancho chiles in hot water for 10 minutes, then blend with vinegar, garlic, cumin, salt, and pepper.

2. Marinate meat for 2–4 hours before grilling.

3. Use extra sauce for basting while grilling.

---

6. Pico de Gallo with Charred Tomatoes

Description:
This twist on traditional Pico de Gallo includes charred tomatoes, adding a smoky depth to the fresh, vibrant flavors. This salsa is perfect as a topping for tacos or as a dip with tortilla chips.

Ingredients:

- 3 tomatoes, halved
- 1/4 cup diced red onion
- 1/4 cup chopped cilantro
- Juice of 1 lime
- Salt and pepper to taste

Instructions:

1. Grill tomato halves until charred, then chop finely.
2. Combine tomatoes with red onion, cilantro, lime juice, salt, and pepper.
3. Serve as a fresh topping or side.

---

7. Spicy Habanero Marinade

Description:
For those who love heat, this Spicy Habanero Marinade adds a fiery kick to meats, especially chicken or shrimp. Habaneros, lime juice, and a hint of honey create a perfect balance of heat and sweetness.

Ingredients:

- 1 habanero pepper, finely chopped
- Juice of 1 lime
- 1 tbsp honey
- 1/4 cup olive oil
- Salt to taste

Instructions:

1. Mix habanero, lime juice, honey, olive oil, and salt in a bowl.
2. Marinate meat or shrimp for 30 minutes to 1 hour before grilling.
3. Grill as desired, brushing with marinade.

8. Garlic-Lime Mojo

Description:
Garlic-Lime Mojo is a tangy, garlic-rich marinade with citrus flavors, ideal for grilled pork or chicken. This Cuban-inspired marinade adds a burst of freshness and works well as both a marinade and a finishing sauce.

Ingredients:

- Juice of 2 limes
- 4 cloves garlic, minced
- 1/4 cup olive oil
- Salt and pepper to taste

Instructions:

1. Combine lime juice, garlic, olive oil, salt, and pepper in a bowl.
2. Marinate meat for 1–2 hours, then grill as desired.
3. Use extra mojo as a drizzle after grilling.

9. Grilled Pineapple Salsa

Description:
Grilled Pineapple Salsa brings a sweet, smoky flavor to grilled meats and seafood. With grilled pineapple, red onion, and

cilantro, it's a tropical, refreshing salsa that complements spicy dishes.

Ingredients:

- 1 cup pineapple slices, grilled and chopped
- 1/4 cup diced red onion
- 1 tbsp chopped cilantro
- Juice of 1 lime
- Salt to taste

Instructions:

1. Grill pineapple slices until charred, then chop into small pieces.
2. Mix with red onion, cilantro, lime juice, and salt.
3. Serve as a salsa for meats or seafood.

---

10. Roasted Tomatillo Salsa

Description:
Roasted Tomatillo Salsa is a tangy, mildly spicy salsa made from roasted tomatillos, jalapeño, and garlic. This versatile salsa is perfect for tacos, burritos, or as a dip for chips.

Ingredients:

- 5 tomatillos, husked and rinsed
- 1 jalapeño, stemmed
- 1 clove garlic
- 1/4 cup fresh cilantro
- Salt to taste

Instructions:

1. Roast tomatillos, jalapeño, and garlic until charred, then let cool.
2. Blend with cilantro and salt until smooth.
3. Serve as a dip or topping for grilled dishes.

Chapter 2: Grilled Vegetables

1. Grilled Corn with Chile-Lime Butter

Description:
Grilled Corn with Chile-Lime Butter is a smoky, spicy, and tangy take on corn on the cob. The chile-lime butter adds a punch of flavor that elevates this simple vegetable, making it a fantastic side dish for any barbecue.

Ingredients:

- 4 ears of corn, husked
- 1/4 cup butter, melted

- 1 tsp chili powder
- Juice of 1 lime
- Salt to taste

Instructions:

1. Grill corn over medium heat, turning occasionally, until charred.
2. Mix melted butter, chili powder, lime juice, and salt.
3. Brush the corn with the chile-lime butter before serving.

2. Charred Poblano Peppers

Description:
Charred Poblano Peppers bring a smoky flavor and mild heat to your meal. These peppers are great served as a side or chopped into salsas for an extra layer of smokiness.

Ingredients:

- 4 poblano peppers
- Olive oil for brushing
- Salt to taste

Instructions:

1. Brush peppers lightly with olive oil and place directly on the grill over medium heat.
2. Grill until the skin is charred and blistered, turning occasionally.
3. Remove from heat, season with salt, and serve whole or sliced.

3. Mexican Grilled Zucchini

Description:
Mexican Grilled Zucchini is seasoned with chili powder and lime, adding a zesty twist to this mild vegetable. It's quick to prepare and pairs well with any grilled meat or as a taco filling.

Ingredients:

- 2 zucchinis, sliced lengthwise
- 2 tbsp olive oil
- 1 tsp chili powder
- Juice of 1/2 lime
- Salt to taste

Instructions:

1. Brush zucchini slices with olive oil and season with chili powder and salt.
2. Grill over medium heat for 3–4 minutes per side.
3. Drizzle with lime juice before serving.

---

4. Roasted Sweet Potatoes with Chipotle

Description:
Roasted Sweet Potatoes with Chipotle offer a sweet and smoky flavor, perfect as a side dish. The chipotle powder adds a spicy kick that balances the natural sweetness of the potatoes.

Ingredients:

- 2 large sweet potatoes, sliced into rounds
- 2 tbsp olive oil
- 1/2 tsp chipotle powder

- Salt to taste

Instructions:

1. Toss sweet potato slices with olive oil, chipotle powder, and salt.
2. Grill over medium heat for 5–7 minutes per side until tender and slightly charred.
3. Serve warm as a flavorful side dish.

---

5. Grilled Avocado with Lime

Description:
Grilled Avocado with Lime is a creamy, smoky appetizer that's quick and easy to prepare. The heat brings out the avocado's natural creaminess, while lime juice adds a refreshing tang.

Ingredients:

- 2 avocados, halved and pitted
- Olive oil for brushing
- Juice of 1/2 lime
- Salt to taste

Instructions:

1. Brush avocado halves with olive oil and place face down on the grill.
2. Grill for 2–3 minutes until charred.
3. Squeeze lime juice over and season with salt before serving.

---

6. Charred Red Onion and Jalapeños

Description:
Charred Red Onion and Jalapeños bring a combination of sweetness and spice. This side is versatile and works well as a topping for tacos or burgers or as a flavorful addition to salsas.

Ingredients:

- 1 large red onion, sliced thickly
- 2 jalapeños, halved lengthwise
- Olive oil for brushing
- Salt to taste

Instructions:

1. Brush onion slices and jalapeños with olive oil and season with salt.
2. Grill over medium heat, turning occasionally, until charred.
3. Serve as a side or chop and use as a topping.

---

7. Smoky Eggplant with Salsa

Description:
Smoky Eggplant with Salsa is a rich, flavorful dish made by charring eggplant and topping it with fresh salsa. The smoky eggplant pairs beautifully with the vibrant, acidic salsa, creating a balanced side.

Ingredients:

- 1 large eggplant, sliced
- Olive oil for brushing
- Salt to taste
- Fresh salsa for topping

Instructions:

1. Brush eggplant slices with olive oil and sprinkle with salt.
2. Grill over medium-high heat until charred and tender, about 4–5 minutes per side.
3. Top with salsa and serve immediately.

---

8. Mexican Grilled Cauliflower

Description:
Mexican Grilled Cauliflower is seasoned with cumin and chili

powder, transforming simple cauliflower into a spicy, smoky delight. This hearty side is perfect for vegetarian grilling.

Ingredients:

- 1 head cauliflower, cut into large florets
- 2 tbsp olive oil
- 1 tsp chili powder
- 1/2 tsp cumin
- Salt to taste

Instructions:

1. Toss cauliflower florets with olive oil, chili powder, cumin, and salt.
2. Grill over medium heat, turning occasionally, until tender and charred, about 10 minutes.
3. Serve as a flavorful side dish.

---

9. Elote (Mexican Street Corn)

Description:
Elote, or Mexican Street Corn, is a classic street food grilled and topped with mayonnaise, cheese, chili powder, and lime. This flavorful corn is a must-try for anyone who loves bold flavors.

Ingredients:

- 4 ears of corn, husked
- 1/4 cup mayonnaise
- 1/4 cup crumbled cotija cheese
- Chili powder to taste

- Juice of 1 lime

Instructions:

1. Grill corn until charred, about 10 minutes, turning occasionally.

2. Spread each ear with mayonnaise, sprinkle with cheese, and dust with chili powder.

3. Squeeze lime juice over before serving.

---

10. Grilled Tomato and Pepper Mix

Description:
Grilled Tomato and Pepper Mix combines juicy tomatoes and bell peppers for a versatile side or taco topping. The charring brings out the natural sweetness of the vegetables, creating a delicious, smoky flavor.

Ingredients:

- 4 tomatoes, halved
- 2 bell peppers, quartered
- Olive oil for brushing
- Salt and pepper to taste

Instructions:

1. Brush tomatoes and bell peppers with olive oil, then season with salt and pepper.

2. Grill over medium heat, turning occasionally, until charred and softened.

3. Serve as a side dish or chop for a taco filling.

Chapter 3: Seafood Specials

1. Grilled Shrimp with Garlic and Cilantro

Description:
Grilled Shrimp with Garlic and Cilantro is a simple yet flavorful dish. Marinated in garlic, cilantro, and lime, these shrimp cook quickly on the grill, making them a perfect appetizer or taco filling.

Ingredients:

- 1 lb shrimp, peeled and deveined
- 3 cloves garlic, minced

- 1/4 cup chopped cilantro
- Juice of 1 lime
- Salt and pepper to taste

Instructions:

1. In a bowl, combine shrimp, garlic, cilantro, lime juice, salt, and pepper. Let marinate for 15–30 minutes.
2. Grill shrimp over medium heat for 2–3 minutes per side, until pink and opaque.
3. Serve as a starter or in tacos.

---

2. Tequila-Lime Marinated Fish

Description:
Tequila-Lime Marinated Fish is a tangy, zesty dish that brings a unique depth of flavor to the grill. This marinade works well with firm fish like mahi-mahi or halibut, giving it a light, citrusy twist.

Ingredients:

- 2 fish fillets (mahi-mahi or halibut)
- 1/4 cup tequila
- Juice of 2 limes
- 2 cloves garlic, minced
- Salt and pepper to taste

Instructions:

1. Combine tequila, lime juice, garlic, salt, and pepper. Marinate fish for 30 minutes.

2. Grill over medium-high heat for 4–5 minutes per side, until cooked through.
   3. Serve with fresh lime wedges.

---

3. Charred Octopus with Achiote

Description:
Charred Octopus with Achiote is a bold dish with a unique flavor profile, thanks to the earthy achiote seasoning. This tender, flavorful octopus is perfect for seafood lovers looking to try something adventurous.

Ingredients:

- 1 lb octopus, cleaned
- 2 tbsp achiote paste
- Juice of 1 lime
- Salt and pepper to taste

Instructions:

1. Boil octopus until tender, then marinate with achiote paste, lime juice, salt, and pepper.
2. Grill over high heat for 3–4 minutes per side until charred.
3. Slice and serve with lime wedges.

---

4. Spicy Grilled Lobster Tails

Description:
Spicy Grilled Lobster Tails are a luxurious treat seasoned with a blend of spices and a hint of chili. This recipe brings out the lobster's natural sweetness with a touch of heat.

Ingredients:

- 2 lobster tails, halved
- 1 tbsp melted butter
- 1 tsp chili powder
- Salt and pepper to taste

Instructions:

1. Brush lobster meat with melted butter, chili powder, salt, and pepper.
2. Grill over medium heat for 5–6 minutes until meat is opaque and slightly charred.
3. Serve with extra melted butter if desired.

---

5. Grilled Fish Tacos

Description:
Grilled Fish Tacos are a Mexican classic, featuring flaky grilled fish with fresh toppings. These tacos are easy to customize and perfect for a light yet flavorful meal.

Ingredients:

- 2 fish fillets (cod or tilapia)
- 1 tbsp olive oil
- Juice of 1 lime
- Salt and pepper to taste
- Tortillas and toppings (cabbage, pico de gallo, lime)

Instructions:

1. Marinate fish with olive oil, lime juice, salt, and pepper.

2. Grill for 3–4 minutes per side until flaky, then break into pieces.

3. Serve in tortillas with desired toppings.

---

6. Cilantro-Lime Grilled Scallops

Description:
Cilantro-Lime Grilled Scallops are fresh and flavorful, with a zesty marinade that complements the delicate scallops. These are quick to cook and make a fantastic appetizer.

Ingredients:
- 1 lb scallops

- 1/4 cup chopped cilantro
- Juice of 1 lime
- 2 tbsp olive oil
- Salt and pepper to taste

Instructions:

1. Marinate scallops with cilantro, lime juice, olive oil, salt, and pepper for 15 minutes.
2. Grill over medium-high heat for 2 minutes per side until cooked through.
3. Serve with additional lime wedges.

---

7. Mexican BBQ Prawns

Description:
Mexican BBQ Prawns are marinated in a blend of spices and then grilled to perfection. These prawns are juicy and full of flavor, making them a crowd-pleasing addition to any barbecue.

Ingredients:

- 1 lb prawns, peeled and deveined
- 1 tsp paprika
- 1/2 tsp cumin
- 1/4 tsp chili powder
- Salt and pepper to taste

Instructions:

1. Toss prawns with paprika, cumin, chili powder, salt, and pepper.

2. Grill over medium heat for 2–3 minutes per side until pink and charred.

3. Serve with a squeeze of lime.

---

8. Grilled Snapper with Mango Salsa

Description:
Grilled Snapper with Mango Salsa combines sweet and savory flavors, with the mango salsa adding a tropical touch to the mild, flaky fish. This dish is refreshing and perfect for warm weather.

Ingredients:

- 1 whole snapper, cleaned
- 1 tbsp olive oil
- Salt and pepper to taste
- Mango salsa for topping

Instructions:

1. Rub snapper with olive oil, salt, and pepper, then grill for 6–8 minutes per side until flaky.

2. Top with mango salsa before serving.

3. Serve with extra salsa on the side.

---

9. Smoked Trout Tostadas

Description:
Smoked Trout Tostadas are crispy, smoky, and packed with flavor. The smoked trout pairs perfectly with fresh toppings, creating a delicious and easy-to-make appetizer.

Ingredients:

- 1 smoked trout fillet
- 4 small tostada shells
- 1/4 cup shredded lettuce
- 1/4 cup diced tomato
- Lime wedges

Instructions:

1. Flake smoked trout and distribute onto tostada shells.
2. Top with lettuce, tomato, and a squeeze of lime.
3. Serve as a flavorful appetizer.

---

10. Citrus-Marinated Shrimp Skewers

Description:
Citrus-Marinated Shrimp Skewers are light, tangy, and perfect for grilling. The citrus marinade enhances the shrimp's natural sweetness, making it a refreshing option for any barbecue.

Ingredients:

- 1 lb shrimp, peeled and deveined
- Juice of 1 orange and 1 lime
- 1 tbsp olive oil
- Salt and pepper to taste

Instructions:

1. Marinate shrimp with orange juice, lime juice, olive oil, salt, and pepper for 15–30 minutes.
2. Thread onto skewers and grill over medium heat for 2–3 minutes per side.

3. Serve with additional lime wedges.

Chapter 4: Chicken Dishes

1. Chipotle-Lime Grilled Chicken

Description:
Chipotle-Lime Grilled Chicken is smoky, spicy, and tangy, making it a flavorful option for summer grilling. The chipotle peppers provide heat, while lime juice adds a refreshing citrus note that complements the chicken beautifully.

Ingredients:

- 4 chicken thighs or breasts
- 2 tbsp chipotle peppers in adobo sauce, minced

- Juice of 1 lime
- 1 tbsp olive oil
- Salt and pepper to taste

Instructions:

1. In a bowl, mix chipotle peppers, lime juice, olive oil, salt, and pepper.
2. Marinate chicken for at least 30 minutes.
3. Grill over medium heat for 6–8 minutes per side, or until cooked through.

---

2. Achiote-Marinated Chicken Thighs

Description:
Achiote-Marinated Chicken Thighs are vibrant and flavorful, thanks to the earthy achiote paste and tangy orange juice. This Yucatán-inspired dish is perfect for those who enjoy bold, traditional Mexican flavors.

Ingredients:

- 4 chicken thighs
- 2 tbsp achiote paste
- 1/4 cup orange juice
- Salt to taste

Instructions:

1. In a bowl, mix achiote paste and orange juice to form a marinade.
2. Coat chicken thighs with the marinade and let sit for at least 1 hour.

3. Grill over medium heat for 6–8 minutes per side, or until cooked through.

---

3. Pollo Asado (Mexican Grilled Chicken)

Description:
Pollo Asado is a classic Mexican grilled chicken, marinated with spices, citrus, and garlic. This simple yet flavorful dish is perfect for serving with rice, beans, or warm tortillas.

Ingredients:

- 4 chicken legs or breasts
- Juice of 2 limes and 1 orange
- 2 cloves garlic, minced
- 1 tsp ground cumin
- Salt and pepper to taste

Instructions:

1. Combine citrus juices, garlic, cumin, salt, and pepper in a bowl.
2. Marinate chicken for at least 1 hour.
3. Grill over medium heat for 8–10 minutes per side until cooked through.

---

4. Tequila and Orange Chicken Skewers

Description:
These Tequila and Orange Chicken Skewers are a flavorful twist on grilled chicken, with the tequila adding a smoky depth and the orange juice a sweet and tangy touch. They make a great appetizer or main dish.

Ingredients:

- 1 lb chicken breast, cubed
- 1/4 cup tequila
- Juice of 1 orange
- Salt and pepper to taste
- Skewers for grilling

Instructions:

1. Marinate chicken with tequila, orange juice, salt, and pepper for 30 minutes.
2. Thread chicken onto skewers.
3. Grill over medium-high heat for 5–7 minutes per side.

---

5. Spicy Grilled Chicken Wings

Description:
Spicy Grilled Chicken Wings are coated in a bold, spicy marinade with chili powder, lime, and garlic. These wings are perfect for sharing at gatherings, adding a fiery kick to any barbecue.

Ingredients:

- 1 lb chicken wings
- 1 tbsp chili powder
- Juice of 1 lime
- 2 cloves garlic, minced
- Salt to taste

Instructions:

1. Mix chili powder, lime juice, garlic, and salt in a bowl.
2. Marinate wings for 30 minutes.
3. Grill over medium heat for 10–12 minutes, turning until crispy.

---

6. Chili-Garlic Chicken Breast

Description:
This Chili-Garlic Chicken Breast is marinated in a flavorful blend of chili paste and garlic, giving it a deep, spicy taste. It's a simple, delicious option for anyone who loves bold flavors.

Ingredients:

- 2 chicken breasts
- 2 tbsp chili paste
- 2 cloves garlic, minced
- Salt to taste

Instructions:

1. Combine chili paste, garlic, and salt.
2. Marinate chicken breasts for 30 minutes.
3. Grill over medium heat for 6–8 minutes per side.

---

7. Mesquite-Smoked Chicken

Description:
Mesquite-Smoked Chicken brings an authentic barbecue flavor to the grill. Marinated with Mexican spices, this chicken is smoked with mesquite wood chips, giving it a unique smoky taste.

Ingredients:

- 4 chicken thighs
- 1 tsp paprika
- 1/2 tsp cumin
- Salt and pepper to taste
- Mesquite wood chips for smoking

Instructions:

1. Season chicken with paprika, cumin, salt, and pepper.
2. Soak mesquite wood chips in water for 30 minutes, then add to the grill.

3. Smoke chicken over low heat for 45 minutes to 1 hour, or until cooked through.

8. Citrus-Glazed Drumsticks

Description:
Citrus-Glazed Drumsticks are sweet, tangy, and perfect for the grill. The glaze caramelizes beautifully, adding a sticky, delicious coating to the drumsticks.

Ingredients:

- 6 chicken drumsticks
- Juice of 1 orange and 1 lime
- 1 tbsp honey
- Salt to taste

Instructions:

1. Combine citrus juices, honey, and salt.
2. Marinate drumsticks for 30 minutes.
3. Grill over medium heat for 10–12 minutes per side, brushing with marinade.

9. Chicken Mole Skewers

Description:
Chicken Mole Skewers are inspired by the rich, chocolatey mole sauce from Mexico. These skewers are a simplified version, offering a blend of spices and a hint of cocoa for a unique, savory taste.

Ingredients:

- 1 lb chicken breast, cubed

- 1/2 tsp cocoa powder
- 1/2 tsp chili powder
- Salt and pepper to taste
- Skewers for grilling

Instructions:

1. Season chicken with cocoa powder, chili powder, salt, and pepper.
2. Thread onto skewers and marinate briefly.
3. Grill over medium heat for 5–7 minutes per side.

---

10. Jalapeño-Marinated Chicken Kebabs

Description:
These Jalapeño-Marinated Chicken Kebabs are spicy and flavorful, with a marinade that brings out the chicken's juiciness and adds a kick from fresh jalapeño.

Ingredients:

- 1 lb chicken breast, cubed
- 1 jalapeño, minced
- Juice of 1 lime
- Salt to taste
- Skewers for grilling

Instructions:

1. Combine chicken, jalapeño, lime juice, and salt. Marinate for 30 minutes.
2. Thread onto skewers.

3. Grill over medium heat for 5–7 minutes per side.

Chapter 5: Pork Delights

1. Grilled Pork Carnitas

Description:
Grilled Pork Carnitas are tender, flavorful pieces of pork with crispy edges. Traditionally slow-cooked, this grilled version captures the deliciously caramelized taste, perfect for tacos or burritos.

Ingredients:

- 1 lb pork shoulder, cubed
- Juice of 1 orange

- 2 cloves garlic, minced
- 1 tsp cumin
- Salt and pepper to taste

Instructions:

1. Marinate pork with orange juice, garlic, cumin, salt, and pepper for 1 hour.
2. Grill over medium-high heat for 8–10 minutes per side until crispy and caramelized.
3. Shred and serve in tortillas with your favorite toppings.

---

2. Spicy BBQ Pork Ribs

Description:
Spicy BBQ Pork Ribs are coated in a spicy rub and grilled until tender. This smoky, spicy dish is ideal for barbecues and brings out the rich flavors of pork ribs.

Ingredients:

- 1 rack pork ribs
- 1 tbsp chili powder
- 1 tsp cumin
- Salt and pepper to taste
- BBQ sauce for brushing

Instructions:

1. Season ribs with chili powder, cumin, salt, and pepper.
2. Grill over low heat for 1.5–2 hours, basting with BBQ sauce every 20 minutes.

3. Serve with extra sauce on the side.

3. Mexican Al Pastor Skewers

Description:
Mexican Al Pastor Skewers bring the traditional flavors of al pastor with pineapple and spices, perfect for grilling. These skewers are juicy, tangy, and ideal for a taco night.

Ingredients:

- 1 lb pork, cubed
- 1/4 cup pineapple juice
- 1 tbsp achiote paste
- Salt and pepper to taste
- Pineapple chunks for skewers

Instructions:

1. Marinate pork with pineapple juice, achiote paste, salt, and pepper for 1 hour.
2. Thread pork and pineapple onto skewers.
3. Grill over medium-high heat for 4–5 minutes per side.

4. Adobo Pork Chops

Description:
Adobo Pork Chops are marinated in a rich adobo sauce, which adds a smoky and tangy flavor. These juicy chops are perfect for a hearty main dish that pairs well with grilled vegetables.

Ingredients:

- 4 pork chops

- 2 tbsp adobo sauce
- 1 tsp garlic powder
- Salt and pepper to taste

Instructions:

1. Rub pork chops with adobo sauce, garlic powder, salt, and pepper.
2. Marinate for 30 minutes.
3. Grill over medium heat for 6–8 minutes per side until fully cooked.

---

5. Chipotle Pork Tenderloin

Description:
Chipotle Pork Tenderloin is marinated with chipotle and lime for a smoky, spicy kick. This tenderloin is juicy, full of flavor, and perfect for slicing and serving with rice or grilled vegetables.

Ingredients:

- 1 pork tenderloin
- 2 tbsp chipotle sauce
- Juice of 1 lime
- Salt and pepper to taste

Instructions:

1. Marinate pork with chipotle sauce, lime juice, salt, and pepper for 1 hour.
2. Grill over medium heat for 12–15 minutes, turning occasionally.
3. Let rest before slicing.

6. Grilled Pork Belly

Description:
Grilled Pork Belly has a rich, crispy texture with a smoky flavor. This cut is perfect for grilling, and the high-fat content results in a melt-in-your-mouth experience with each bite.

Ingredients:

- 1 lb pork belly, sliced
- Salt and pepper to taste
- Optional: chili powder for extra spice

Instructions:

1. Season pork belly with salt, pepper, and chili powder if desired.
2. Grill over medium-high heat for 5–7 minutes per side until crispy.
3. Serve hot as a side or in tacos.

7. Orange and Chili-Glazed Pork

Description:
Orange and Chili-Glazed Pork is a sweet and spicy dish with a citrus glaze that caramelizes beautifully on the grill. The orange juice adds sweetness, while the chili gives it a kick.

Ingredients:

- 1 lb pork chops or pork loin
- Juice of 1 orange
- 1 tsp chili flakes
- Salt to taste

Instructions:

1. Mix orange juice, chili flakes, and salt to create a glaze.
2. Marinate pork for 30 minutes.
3. Grill over medium heat, basting with glaze, for 6–8 minutes per side.

8. Mesquite-Smoked Pork Shoulder

Description:
Mesquite-Smoked Pork Shoulder is slow-cooked over mesquite wood chips for a deep, smoky flavor. This cut is tender and juicy, ideal for shredding and serving as a main dish.

Ingredients:

- 1 lb pork shoulder
- 1 tbsp smoked paprika
- Salt and pepper to taste
- Mesquite wood chips for smoking

Instructions:

1. Rub pork with smoked paprika, salt, and pepper.
2. Add soaked mesquite wood chips to the grill and smoke pork shoulder over low heat for 2–3 hours.
3. Shred and serve as desired.

---

9. Marinated Pork Skewers

Description:
Marinated Pork Skewers are tender and flavorful, perfect for quick grilling. The marinade combines spices and lime juice, making these skewers juicy and vibrant.

Ingredients:

- 1 lb pork, cubed
- 1 tsp cumin
- Juice of 1 lime
- Salt and pepper to taste
- Skewers for grilling

Instructions:

1. Marinate pork with cumin, lime juice, salt, and pepper for 30 minutes.

2. Thread onto skewers and grill over medium-high heat for 5–7 minutes per side.
3. Serve hot.

---

10. Spicy BBQ Sausages

Description:
Spicy BBQ Sausages are packed with flavor, ideal for grilling. They're seasoned with chili powder and garlic for a kick and are perfect as a main dish or added to tacos.

Ingredients:

- 4 pork sausages
- 1 tsp chili powder
- 1 tsp garlic powder
- BBQ sauce for brushing

Instructions:

1. Sprinkle sausages with chili powder and garlic powder.
2. Grill over medium heat, turning occasionally, for 8–10 minutes.
3. Brush with BBQ sauce during the last few minutes of grilling.

Chapter 6: Beef Favorites

1. Grilled Carne Asada

Description:
Carne Asada is a classic Mexican dish of grilled, marinated beef, known for its bold flavors. This recipe uses lime, garlic, and spices to infuse the beef with vibrant flavors, perfect for tacos or serving with rice and beans.

Ingredients:

- 1 lb skirt or flank steak
- Juice of 2 limes

- 3 cloves garlic, minced
- 1 tsp ground cumin
- Salt and pepper to taste

Instructions:

1. Marinate steak with lime juice, garlic, cumin, salt, and pepper for at least 1 hour.
2. Grill over high heat for 3–4 minutes per side until desired doneness.
3. Slice thinly and serve in tortillas or as a main dish.

---

2. Beef Fajitas

Description:
Beef Fajitas are a crowd-pleaser with tender, marinated strips of beef grilled alongside bell peppers and onions. These fajitas are flavorful and perfect for wrapping in tortillas with your favorite toppings.

Ingredients:

- 1 lb beef sirloin or flank steak, sliced
- 1 red bell pepper, sliced
- 1 green bell pepper, sliced
- 1 onion, sliced
- 2 tbsp olive oil
- Salt and pepper to taste

Instructions:

1. Toss beef, bell peppers, and onion with olive oil, salt, and pepper.

2. Grill over medium-high heat for 5–6 minutes, stirring occasionally.
3. Serve with warm tortillas and toppings of choice.

3. Tequila-Marinated Steak

Description:
Tequila-Marinated Steak adds a unique twist with a blend of tequila, lime, and spices that infuse the beef with a hint of smoky sweetness. It's a delicious way to elevate any barbecue meal.

Ingredients:

- 1 lb sirloin steak
- 1/4 cup tequila
- Juice of 1 lime
- 2 cloves garlic, minced
- Salt and pepper to taste

Instructions:

1. Marinate steak with tequila, lime juice, garlic, salt, and pepper for at least 1 hour.
2. Grill over medium-high heat for 4–5 minutes per side.
3. Let rest before slicing and serving.

4. Barbacoa-Style Grilled Beef

Description:
Inspired by traditional barbacoa, this grilled version uses a blend of spices, lime, and garlic to season the beef. The result is tender, flavorful meat perfect for tacos or burritos.

Ingredients:

- 1 lb beef chuck or brisket
- 2 tsp ground cumin
- 1 tsp smoked paprika
- Juice of 1 lime
- Salt and pepper to taste

Instructions:

1. Season beef with cumin, smoked paprika, lime juice, salt, and pepper.
2. Grill over low heat for 2–3 hours until tender, turning occasionally.
3. Shred and serve in tacos or as a main dish.

---

5. Chipotle Steak Skewers

Description:
These Chipotle Steak Skewers are smoky, spicy, and easy to prepare. The chipotle marinade adds depth of flavor, making them a hit at any barbecue gathering.

Ingredients:

- 1 lb beef sirloin, cubed
- 2 tbsp chipotle sauce
- Salt and pepper to taste
- Skewers for grilling

Instructions:

1. Marinate beef cubes with chipotle sauce, salt, and pepper for 30 minutes.
2. Thread onto skewers and grill over medium-high heat for 4–5 minutes per side.
3. Serve hot with your favorite dipping sauce.

---

6. Ancho Chili-Marinated Flank Steak

Description:
Ancho Chili-Marinated Flank Steak offers a deep, smoky flavor thanks to ancho chili powder. This recipe is perfect for those who enjoy a bit of heat with their grilled beef.

Ingredients:

- 1 lb flank steak
- 2 tsp ancho chili powder
- Juice of 1 lime
- 1 tbsp olive oil
- Salt and pepper to taste

Instructions:

1. Marinate steak with ancho chili powder, lime juice, olive oil, salt, and pepper for at least 1 hour.
2. Grill over medium-high heat for 5–6 minutes per side.
3. Let rest before slicing and serving.

---

7. Grilled Beef Tacos

Description:
Grilled Beef Tacos are a simple yet flavorful dish, with seasoned beef that's perfect for filling tortillas. Add toppings like fresh cilantro, onions, and salsa for an authentic Mexican experience.

Ingredients:

- 1 lb beef sirloin, sliced
- 2 tbsp olive oil
- Salt and pepper to taste
- Tortillas and toppings (cilantro, onion, salsa)

Instructions:

1. Toss beef with olive oil, salt, and pepper.
2. Grill over medium-high heat for 4–5 minutes per side.

3. Serve in tortillas with desired toppings.

8. Smoky Beef Ribs

Description:
Smoky Beef Ribs are seasoned with a blend of spices and slow-grilled for a rich, tender result. This recipe is ideal for fans of smoky, fall-off-the-bone ribs.

Ingredients:

- 1 rack beef ribs
- 1 tbsp smoked paprika
- 1 tsp ground cumin
- Salt and pepper to taste
- BBQ sauce for basting

Instructions:

1. Season ribs with smoked paprika, cumin, salt, and pepper.
2. Grill over low heat for 1.5–2 hours, basting with BBQ sauce every 20 minutes.
3. Serve with extra sauce on the side.

9. Marinated Beef Short Ribs

Description:
Marinated Beef Short Ribs are infused with a savory marinade that makes them tender and flavorful. Grilled to perfection, they're an excellent choice for a hearty main dish.

Ingredients:

- 1 lb beef short ribs
- 1/4 cup soy sauce
- 1 tbsp brown sugar
- 2 cloves garlic, minced
- Salt and pepper to taste

Instructions:

1. Marinate short ribs with soy sauce, brown sugar, garlic, salt, and pepper for at least 1 hour.
2. Grill over medium-high heat for 6–8 minutes per side.
3. Serve hot.

---

10. Cilantro and Garlic Beef Skewers

Description:
Cilantro and Garlic Beef Skewers are aromatic and flavorful, with the fresh taste of cilantro and the savory touch of garlic. These skewers are perfect for grilling and sharing.

Ingredients:

- 1 lb beef sirloin, cubed
- 1/4 cup chopped cilantro
- 3 cloves garlic, minced
- Salt and pepper to taste
- Skewers for grilling

Instructions:

1. Toss beef cubes with cilantro, garlic, salt, and pepper.

2. Thread onto skewers and grill over medium-high heat for 4–5 minutes per side.
3. Serve as an appetizer or main dish.

Chapter 7: Tacos and Tostadas

1. Grilled Fish Tacos with Lime Crema

Description:
Grilled Fish Tacos with Lime Crema are light and flavorful, featuring seasoned grilled fish topped with a creamy lime sauce. These tacos are refreshing and perfect for warm-weather grilling.

Ingredients:

- 1 lb white fish fillets (e.g., cod or tilapia)
- 1 tbsp olive oil
- Salt and pepper to taste

- 1/4 cup sour cream
- Juice of 1 lime
- Tortillas and toppings (cabbage, cilantro)

Instructions:

1. Brush fish with olive oil, salt, and pepper, then grill over medium heat for 3–4 minutes per side.
2. Mix sour cream with lime juice to create the lime crema.
3. Serve fish in tortillas with lime crema and desired toppings.

---

2. BBQ Pork Tacos

Description:
BBQ Pork Tacos feature tender grilled pork coated in a smoky BBQ sauce, making them a flavorful option for taco night. These tacos are best served with crunchy slaw and fresh cilantro.

Ingredients:

- 1 lb pork shoulder, shredded
- 1/4 cup BBQ sauce
- Salt and pepper to taste
- Tortillas and toppings (slaw, cilantro)

Instructions:

1. Season pork with salt and pepper, then grill over medium heat until fully cooked.
2. Shred pork and mix with BBQ sauce.
3. Serve in tortillas with slaw and cilantro.

3. Smoky Grilled Chicken Tacos

Description:
Smoky Grilled Chicken Tacos are made with marinated chicken that's grilled to perfection. The smoky flavor pairs well with fresh toppings, making these tacos a crowd-pleaser.

Ingredients:

- 1 lb chicken thighs, sliced
- 1 tsp smoked paprika
- Salt and pepper to taste
- Tortillas and toppings (lettuce, salsa)

Instructions:

1. Season chicken with smoked paprika, salt, and pepper, then grill over medium heat for 5–6 minutes per side.
2. Slice grilled chicken and serve in tortillas with your choice of toppings.

4. Carne Asada Tacos

Description:
Carne Asada Tacos feature thinly sliced grilled beef, marinated for maximum flavor. These tacos are perfect with simple toppings like onion, cilantro, and lime.

Ingredients:

- 1 lb flank steak
- Juice of 1 lime
- 2 cloves garlic, minced

- Salt and pepper to taste
- Tortillas and toppings (onion, cilantro)

Instructions:

1. Marinate steak with lime juice, garlic, salt, and pepper for at least 30 minutes.
2. Grill over high heat for 3–4 minutes per side, then slice thinly.
3. Serve in tortillas with onion, cilantro, and a squeeze of lime.

---

5. Shrimp Tacos with Mango Salsa

Description:
Shrimp Tacos with Mango Salsa are light, zesty, and tropical. The grilled shrimp pairs wonderfully with the fresh mango salsa, making these tacos a refreshing choice.

Ingredients:

- 1 lb shrimp, peeled and deveined
- Salt and pepper to taste
- 1 mango, diced
- 1/4 cup diced red onion
- 1 tbsp chopped cilantro
- Juice of 1 lime

Instructions:

1. Grill shrimp over medium heat for 2–3 minutes per side, seasoned with salt and pepper.

2. Combine mango, red onion, cilantro, and lime juice to make the salsa.

3. Serve shrimp in tortillas with mango salsa.

---

6. Grilled Veggie Tostadas

Description:
Grilled Veggie Tostadas are topped with seasoned, charred vegetables, offering a healthy and satisfying option. These tostadas are customizable and ideal for veggie lovers.

Ingredients:
- 1 zucchini, sliced

- 1 bell pepper, sliced
- 1/4 cup black beans
- Salt and pepper to taste
- Tostada shells and toppings (avocado, salsa)

Instructions:

1. Grill zucchini and bell pepper over medium heat until tender, then chop.
2. Top tostada shells with black beans, grilled veggies, and toppings.
3. Serve immediately.

---

7. BBQ Beef Tacos

Description:
BBQ Beef Tacos are filled with grilled, marinated beef coated in BBQ sauce. These hearty tacos are ideal for beef lovers and pair well with pickled onions.

Ingredients:

- 1 lb beef sirloin, sliced
- 1/4 cup BBQ sauce
- Salt and pepper to taste
- Tortillas and toppings (pickled onions, cilantro)

Instructions:

1. Grill beef over medium-high heat, seasoned with salt and pepper.
2. Slice and coat with BBQ sauce, then serve in tortillas with toppings.

8. Chorizo Tacos

Description:
Chorizo Tacos are spicy, savory, and bursting with flavor. The grilled chorizo is rich and pairs well with simple toppings like onion and cilantro.

Ingredients:

- 1 lb chorizo sausage
- Tortillas and toppings (onion, cilantro, lime)

Instructions:

1. Grill chorizo over medium heat until fully cooked, then slice or crumble.
2. Serve in tortillas with chopped onion, cilantro, and a squeeze of lime.

---

9. Charred Avocado Tostadas

Description:
Charred Avocado Tostadas bring a unique flavor with smoky, grilled avocado. Topped with fresh salsa and cotija cheese, these tostadas are a creamy, delicious treat.

Ingredients:

- 2 avocados, halved and pitted
- Salt to taste
- Tostada shells and toppings (salsa, cotija cheese)

Instructions:

1. Grill avocado halves for 2–3 minutes until lightly charred.

2. Scoop avocado onto tostada shells, season with salt, and add toppings.

3. Serve immediately.

---

10. Street-Style Steak Tacos

Description:
Street-Style Steak Tacos are inspired by classic Mexican street food, featuring grilled, seasoned steak in warm tortillas. These tacos are perfect with chopped onion, cilantro, and a squeeze of lime.

Ingredients:

- 1 lb skirt steak
- Salt and pepper to taste
- Tortillas and toppings (onion, cilantro, lime)

Instructions:

1. Season steak with salt and pepper, then grill over medium-high heat for 4–5 minutes per side.

2. Slice thinly and serve in tortillas with onion, cilantro, and lime.

Chapter 8: Burgers and Sandwiches

1. Mexican Chorizo Burgers

Description:
Mexican Chorizo Burgers are a spicy twist on a classic burger, combining ground beef with chorizo for added flavor. Topped with avocado and cilantro, these burgers bring a bold taste that's sure to impress.

Ingredients:

- 1/2 lb ground beef
- 1/2 lb Mexican chorizo, casings removed

- Salt and pepper to taste
- Burger buns and toppings (avocado, cilantro)

Instructions:

1. Mix ground beef and chorizo, season with salt and pepper, and form into patties.
2. Grill over medium-high heat for 4–5 minutes per side until fully cooked.
3. Serve on buns with avocado, cilantro, and your favorite toppings.

---

2. Chipotle Chicken Sandwiches

Description:
Chipotle Chicken Sandwiches feature marinated grilled chicken with a smoky, spicy chipotle flavor. Perfectly paired with lettuce and tomato, this sandwich is satisfying and flavorful.

Ingredients:

- 2 chicken breasts
- 2 tbsp chipotle sauce
- Salt and pepper to taste
- Buns and toppings (lettuce, tomato)

Instructions:

1. Marinate chicken in chipotle sauce, salt, and pepper for 30 minutes.
2. Grill over medium heat for 5–6 minutes per side until cooked through.
3. Serve on buns with lettuce, tomato, and additional chipotle sauce.

3. Grilled Fish Po' Boy

Description:
Grilled Fish Po' Boy is a Mexican-inspired version of the classic sandwich, featuring grilled fish fillets and topped with fresh pico de gallo and spicy mayo for extra flavor.

Ingredients:

- 2 fish fillets (tilapia or cod)
- Salt and pepper to taste
- Sub rolls and toppings (pico de gallo, spicy mayo)

Instructions:

1. Season fish with salt and pepper, then grill over medium-high heat for 3–4 minutes per side.
2. Serve in sub rolls, topped with pico de gallo and a drizzle of spicy mayo.

4. Spicy BBQ Pork Sandwich

Description:
Spicy BBQ Pork Sandwich is filled with shredded grilled pork, mixed with smoky BBQ sauce and topped with crunchy coleslaw. This sandwich is full of flavor and perfect for BBQ lovers.

Ingredients:

- 1 lb pork shoulder, shredded
- 1/4 cup BBQ sauce
- Buns and toppings (coleslaw)

Instructions:

1. Grill pork shoulder over medium heat until fully cooked, then shred.
2. Toss shredded pork with BBQ sauce.
3. Serve on buns with a topping of coleslaw.

---

5. Jalapeño Beef Burgers

Description:
Jalapeño Beef Burgers offer a spicy kick, with diced jalapeños mixed into the beef. Topped with cheese and spicy mayo, these burgers are great for heat lovers.

Ingredients:

- 1 lb ground beef
- 1 jalapeño, diced
- Salt and pepper to taste
- Burger buns and toppings (cheese, spicy mayo)

Instructions:

1. Mix ground beef with diced jalapeño, salt, and pepper, then form into patties.
2. Grill over medium-high heat for 4–5 minutes per side until fully cooked.
3. Serve on buns with cheese and spicy mayo.

---

6. Grilled Veggie Burger

Description:
Grilled Veggie Burger is packed with flavor, featuring a patty made from black beans, corn, and spices. Topped with avocado and salsa, it's a delicious vegetarian option.

Ingredients:

- 1 cup black beans, mashed
- 1/4 cup corn
- 1/2 tsp chili powder
- Salt and pepper to taste
- Burger buns and toppings (avocado, salsa)

Instructions:

1. Mix black beans, corn, chili powder, salt, and pepper, then form into patties.

2. Grill over medium heat for 3–4 minutes per side.

3. Serve on buns with avocado and salsa.

---

7. Shrimp and Avocado Sandwich

Description:
Shrimp and Avocado Sandwich is light and refreshing, made with grilled shrimp, creamy avocado, and fresh cilantro. This sandwich is perfect for a sunny day.

Ingredients:

- 1/2 lb shrimp, peeled and deveined
- Salt and pepper to taste
- Rolls and toppings (avocado, cilantro)

Instructions:

1. Season shrimp with salt and pepper, then grill over medium heat for 2–3 minutes per side.

2. Serve on rolls with slices of avocado and a sprinkle of cilantro.

---

8. BBQ Chicken Torta

Description:
BBQ Chicken Torta is a Mexican-style sandwich featuring grilled chicken coated in BBQ sauce. Topped with lettuce, tomatoes, and a smear of mayo, this torta is satisfying and flavorful.

Ingredients:

- 2 chicken breasts
- 1/4 cup BBQ sauce
- Torta rolls and toppings (lettuce, tomato, mayo)

Instructions:

1. Grill chicken, brushing with BBQ sauce, for 5–6 minutes per side.
2. Serve on torta rolls with lettuce, tomato, and mayo.

---

9. Carne Asada Sandwich

Description:
Carne Asada Sandwich features thinly sliced grilled steak, marinated and full of flavor. This sandwich is perfect with fresh avocado, onion, and a squeeze of lime.

Ingredients:

- 1 lb skirt steak
- Juice of 1 lime
- Salt and pepper to taste
- Rolls and toppings (avocado, onion, lime)

Instructions:

1. Marinate steak with lime juice, salt, and pepper, then grill for 3–4 minutes per side.
2. Slice thinly and serve on rolls with avocado, onion, and lime.

---

10. Grilled Cheese Quesadilla Burger

Description:
Grilled Cheese Quesadilla Burger combines the classic burger with a quesadilla twist. The burger is sandwiched between two cheesy quesadillas, adding a Mexican flair to every bite.

Ingredients:

- 1 lb ground beef, formed into patties
- 4 tortillas
- 1 cup shredded cheese
- Salt and pepper to taste

Instructions:

1. Grill burger patties for 4–5 minutes per side, seasoned with salt and pepper.
2. Grill tortillas with cheese to make quesadillas.
3. Place burger between two quesadillas and serve.

Chapter 9: Sides and Street Foods

1. Mexican Grilled Corn Salad

Description:
Mexican Grilled Corn Salad is a vibrant side made with grilled corn, lime, and fresh herbs. It's a deliciously tangy, smoky dish that pairs well with any grilled meat or can be enjoyed as a standalone appetizer.

Ingredients:

- 4 ears of corn, grilled and kernels removed
- 1/4 cup chopped cilantro

- Juice of 1 lime
- 1/4 cup crumbled cotija cheese
- Salt and pepper to taste

Instructions:

1. In a bowl, mix grilled corn, cilantro, lime juice, cotija cheese, salt, and pepper.
2. Toss until well combined and serve chilled or at room temperature.

---

2. Smoky Refried Beans

Description:
Smoky Refried Beans are a classic Mexican side made even better with a hint of smokiness. Perfect as a side dish or a filling for tacos and burritos, these beans are creamy and full of flavor.

Ingredients:

- 1 can pinto beans, drained
- 1/2 tsp smoked paprika
- 1 clove garlic, minced
- Salt to taste

Instructions:

1. Mash beans in a skillet over medium heat with garlic, smoked paprika, and salt.
2. Stir occasionally until heated through and creamy.
3. Serve as a side or as a filling.

3. Charred Jalapeño Peppers

Description:
Charred Jalapeño Peppers add a smoky, spicy kick to any meal. These are perfect as a garnish, a side dish, or chopped into salsas for extra heat.

Ingredients:

- 6 whole jalapeño peppers
- Olive oil for brushing
- Salt to taste

Instructions:

1. Brush jalapeños with olive oil and grill over high heat until charred.
2. Sprinkle with salt and serve whole or sliced as a topping.

---

4. Grilled Plantains with Honey

Description:
Grilled Plantains with Honey are a sweet, caramelized treat that pairs beautifully with savory grilled dishes. The honey glaze enhances the plantain's natural sweetness, making it a crowd-pleasing side.

Ingredients:

- 2 ripe plantains, sliced lengthwise
- 2 tbsp honey
- 1 tsp cinnamon (optional)

Instructions:

1. Brush plantain slices with honey and sprinkle with cinnamon if desired.

2. Grill over medium heat for 2–3 minutes per side until caramelized.

3. Serve warm.

---

5. Mexican Rice with Grilled Tomatoes

Description:
Mexican Rice with Grilled Tomatoes is a savory, aromatic side made with fluffy rice and smoky grilled tomatoes. This dish is a flavorful accompaniment to any main course.

Ingredients:

- 1 cup long-grain rice
- 2 grilled tomatoes, chopped
- 1 clove garlic, minced
- Salt to taste

Instructions:

1. Sauté garlic in a pan, add rice, and cook until lightly toasted.
2. Stir in grilled tomatoes and water, then cover and simmer until rice is cooked.
3. Season with salt before serving.

---

6. Roasted Poblano Guacamole

Description:
Roasted Poblano Guacamole combines creamy avocado with smoky poblano peppers for a unique, flavorful dip. It's perfect as a side or as a topping for tacos and grilled meats.

Ingredients:

- 2 avocados, mashed
- 1 roasted poblano pepper, chopped
- Juice of 1 lime
- Salt to taste

Instructions:

1. Combine mashed avocado with roasted poblano, lime juice, and salt.
2. Mix until well combined and serve as a dip or topping.

---

7. Street-Style Grilled Corn

Description:
Street-Style Grilled Corn, or "Elote," is a popular Mexican street food. Topped with mayo, cheese, and chili powder, this corn is savory, spicy, and utterly delicious.

Ingredients:

- 4 ears of corn, husked
- 1/4 cup mayonnaise
- 1/4 cup crumbled cotija cheese
- Chili powder to taste
- Lime wedges for serving

Instructions:

1. Grill corn over medium heat until charred, about 10 minutes.
2. Spread mayo over corn, sprinkle with cheese and chili powder, and serve with lime wedges.

---

8. Grilled Cactus Salad

Description:
Grilled Cactus Salad, or "Nopalitos," is a tangy and refreshing side made with grilled cactus paddles, tomatoes, and onions. It's a unique and nutritious addition to any Mexican meal.

Ingredients:

- 2 cactus paddles, grilled and sliced
- 1 tomato, diced
- 1/4 onion, chopped
- Juice of 1 lime
- Salt to taste

Instructions:

1. Combine grilled cactus, tomato, onion, lime juice, and salt in a bowl.
2. Toss well and serve chilled or at room temperature.

---

9. BBQ Elote Fritters

Description:
BBQ Elote Fritters are a fun twist on classic Mexican street corn, blending grilled corn with batter and frying until crispy. These fritters are flavorful, crispy, and perfect for snacking.

Ingredients:

- 1 cup grilled corn kernels
- 1/4 cup flour
- 1 egg, beaten
- 1/4 cup crumbled cotija cheese
- Salt to taste

Instructions:

1. Mix corn, flour, egg, cheese, and salt to create a batter.
2. Drop spoonfuls onto a hot, oiled skillet and fry until golden brown on both sides.

3. Serve warm.

---

10. Charred Tomato Salsa

Description:
Charred Tomato Salsa has a smoky depth of flavor from grilled tomatoes, making it a delicious dip or taco topping. This salsa is quick to make and adds a bold taste to any dish.

Ingredients:
- 4 tomatoes, halved and grilled
- 1/4 cup chopped cilantro
- 1 clove garlic, minced
- Salt to taste

Instructions:
1. Grill tomato halves until charred, then chop.
2. Mix with cilantro, garlic, and salt, adjusting seasoning as desired.
3. Serve as a salsa for chips or as a topping for grilled dishes.

Chapter 10: Desserts and Drinks

1. Grilled Pineapple with Cinnamon

Description:
Grilled Pineapple with Cinnamon is a simple yet delicious dessert, where the natural sweetness of pineapple caramelizes on the grill, and a sprinkle of cinnamon adds warmth and depth.

Ingredients:

- 1 pineapple, peeled and sliced
- 1 tbsp cinnamon

- Honey for drizzling (optional)

Instructions:

1. Sprinkle pineapple slices with cinnamon.
2. Grill over medium-high heat for 3–4 minutes per side until caramelized.
3. Drizzle with honey before serving if desired.

---

2. BBQ Mango Skewers

Description:
BBQ Mango Skewers are a sweet, tropical treat that grills quickly and brings out the mango's natural sugars. Perfect for summer, these skewers are lightly caramelized and bursting with flavor.

Ingredients:

- 2 mangoes, peeled and cubed
- Wooden skewers
- 1 tbsp lime juice

Instructions:

1. Thread mango cubes onto skewers and brush with lime juice.
2. Grill over medium heat for 2–3 minutes per side until lightly charred.
3. Serve warm as a refreshing dessert.

---

3. Mexican Grilled Bananas

Description:
Mexican Grilled Bananas are a comforting, warm dessert with a hint of spice. Grilled until soft and topped with cinnamon and a drizzle of chocolate, they're an indulgent yet easy treat.

Ingredients:

- 4 bananas, peeled and halved lengthwise
- 1 tsp cinnamon
- Melted chocolate for drizzling

Instructions:

1. Sprinkle bananas with cinnamon.
2. Grill over medium heat for 2–3 minutes per side until softened.
3. Drizzle with melted chocolate before serving.

---

4. Sweet Corn Custard

Description:
Sweet Corn Custard is a unique dessert that combines the natural sweetness of corn with a creamy custard texture. It's lightly grilled to add a smoky flavor, making it a comforting and unusual treat.

Ingredients:

- 1 cup corn kernels
- 1/2 cup milk
- 1/4 cup sugar
- 2 eggs, beaten

Instructions:

1. Blend corn, milk, sugar, and eggs until smooth.
2. Pour mixture into a heatproof dish and place on a low grill for 20–25 minutes until set.
3. Serve warm or chilled.

---

5. Lime and Coconut Grilled Fruit

Description:
Lime and Coconut Grilled Fruit is a tropical dessert that's easy to make and full of flavor. The lime juice adds tanginess, while the coconut provides sweetness, complementing grilled fruits like pineapple and peaches.

Ingredients:

- Assorted fruits (pineapple, peaches, etc.), sliced
- Juice of 1 lime
- 2 tbsp shredded coconut

Instructions:

1. Brush fruits with lime juice and sprinkle with shredded coconut.
2. Grill over medium-high heat for 2–3 minutes per side until caramelized.
3. Serve warm as a tropical treat.

---

6. Grilled Churros

Description:

Grilled Churros are a fun twist on the classic Mexican treat. These skewered churro sticks are brushed with cinnamon sugar and grilled until warm, perfect for dipping in chocolate sauce.

Ingredients:

- 8 churro sticks, skewered
- 1/4 cup melted butter
- 2 tbsp cinnamon sugar

Instructions:

1. Brush churros with melted butter, then coat with cinnamon sugar.

2. Grill over medium heat for 2–3 minutes, turning until warmed and slightly crispy.

3. Serve with chocolate sauce for dipping.

---

7. Charred Watermelon Salad

Description:
Charred Watermelon Salad is a refreshing mix of sweet and savory flavors, with the smoky grilled watermelon paired with mint and a touch of lime for a unique summer dessert.

Ingredients:

- 4 watermelon wedges
- Fresh mint leaves, chopped
- Juice of 1 lime

Instructions:

1. Grill watermelon wedges over high heat for 1–2 minutes per side until charred.
2. Cut into cubes, toss with mint and lime juice, and serve chilled.

---

8. Smoky Mezcal Margarita

Description:
Smoky Mezcal Margarita is a bold, refreshing drink with the earthy, smoky flavors of mezcal. Combined with lime and a hint of sweetness, it's a perfect pairing for grilled dishes.

Ingredients:

- 2 oz mezcal
- 1 oz lime juice

- 1/2 oz agave syrup
- Salt for rim (optional)

Instructions:

1. Rim glass with salt if desired.
2. Shake mezcal, lime juice, and agave syrup with ice.
3. Pour into a glass and garnish with a lime wedge.

---

9. Pineapple Jalapeño Mocktail

Description:
The Pineapple Jalapeño Mocktail combines sweet pineapple with a hint of jalapeño heat for a refreshing, non-alcoholic drink that's perfect for summer BBQs.

Ingredients:

- 1 cup pineapple juice
- 1/2 jalapeño, sliced
- Sparkling water
- Ice cubes

Instructions:

1. Muddle jalapeño slices in a glass, then add pineapple juice and ice.
2. Top with sparkling water and stir.
3. Garnish with a pineapple slice.

---

10. Citrus Mint Agua Fresca

Description:

Citrus Mint Agua Fresca is a light, refreshing drink with fresh mint and a mix of citrus flavors. This agua fresca is ideal for cooling down on a hot day and pairs well with grilled foods.

Ingredients:

- 1 orange, juiced
- 1 lime, juiced
- 1/4 cup fresh mint leaves
- 2 cups water
- Ice cubes

Instructions:

1. Combine orange juice, lime juice, mint leaves, and water in a pitcher.
2. Serve over ice and garnish with extra mint.

Appendices and Tips
Mastering Mexican Grilling and BBQ

1. **Flavorful Marinades and Rubs**
   The key to Mexican grilling often lies in marinades and rubs. Many dishes, from carne asada to adobo pork, rely on bold flavors from ingredients like citrus juices, garlic, and herbs. Citrus-based marinades with lime or orange add acidity that tenderizes meats and enhances natural flavors. For an even richer taste, combine citrus with ingredients like tequila or achiote paste, which bring unique depth and earthy notes to the dishes. Rubs are equally essential for an outer crust, so consider using spices like chili powder, cumin, and smoked paprika to enhance flavor without overpowering the natural taste of the meat.

2. **Using Fresh Herbs and Spices**
   Herbs like cilantro and oregano, along with fresh garlic and onion, form the backbone of Mexican grilling. Cilantro is commonly used in salsas, marinades, and garnishes. Try adding fresh herbs toward the end of cooking to preserve their flavors, or use them as part of a final garnish for a burst of freshness. Spices such as cumin, smoked paprika, and chili powder add earthiness and smokiness, while dried oregano adds a unique Mexican touch to many dishes.

3. **Adding Smoke for Depth**
   Mexican BBQ often incorporates smoky flavors, especially with ingredients like chipotle and mesquite. If you're using a charcoal grill, adding soaked wood chips (like mesquite or hickory) can impart this rich smokiness. For an even deeper smoky flavor, cook at a lower temperature and cover the grill, allowing the smoke to infuse the food. Smoked paprika or chipotle

powder is a convenient way to add smokiness without additional equipment.

Spice Guide for Mexican Grilling

1. **Chili Powder and Ancho Chili Powder**
   Chili powder, commonly a blend of spices, is versatile for seasoning meats and veggies. Ancho chili powder, made from dried poblano peppers, adds a sweet, smoky heat and is perfect for rubs or marinades.

2. **Cumin**
   With its earthy, nutty flavor, cumin is a cornerstone of Mexican BBQ. It pairs well with chili powders, garlic, and lime, making it ideal for marinades and rubs. Use ground cumin for a strong, aromatic kick, or toast whole cumin seeds to release their oils and enhance flavor.

3. **Paprika and Smoked Paprika**
   Both regular and smoked paprika bring mild sweetness, with smoked paprika adding a smoky dimension that complements grilled meats. Smoked paprika is particularly effective in BBQ rubs and chili-based sauces.

4. **Achiote (Annatto) Paste**
   Achiote paste, made from ground annatto seeds, brings a bright red color and earthy flavor, often found in Yucatán-style dishes like al pastor or cochinita pibil. Its subtle spice and slightly bitter taste work well when paired with citrus in marinades.

5. **Mexican Oregano**
   More pungent and less sweet than Mediterranean oregano, Mexican oregano pairs well with chili and lime flavors. It's ideal in salsas, marinades, and even rubs for

pork and beef dishes, bringing a distinct herbaceous flavor.

6. **Garlic and Onion Powders**
While fresh garlic and onions are frequently used, their powdered forms add a concentrated flavor that's easy to blend into rubs or marinades.

Essential Grilling Techniques

1. **Direct and Indirect Grilling**
Understanding direct and indirect grilling is essential for mastering Mexican BBQ. For meats like carne asada or shrimp skewers, grilling directly over high heat sears the meat, giving it a caramelized crust. However, tougher cuts like pork shoulder benefit from indirect heat, allowing them to cook slowly and tenderize. Simply place the coals to one side of the grill to create zones and move food between high and low heat as needed.

2. **Controlling Temperature**
Temperature control is critical for perfect grilling results. For searing, aim for a high temperature of around 400–450°F. For slower cooking, especially for ribs or large cuts, maintain a steady temperature between 250–300°F. Keep an eye on the grill vents, opening them to increase airflow and heat, or closing to maintain a lower temperature.

3. **Using a Meat Thermometer**
To ensure meat is cooked through while staying juicy, use a meat thermometer to check the internal temperature. For beef and pork, a temperature of around 145°F is ideal for medium-rare, while chicken should reach 165°F. This is especially useful when grilling thick cuts, ensuring they're cooked evenly.

4. **Letting Meat Rest**
   Once removed from the grill, allow meat to rest for a few minutes to retain its juices. This resting period allows the juices to redistribute, resulting in tender and flavorful meat. For thicker cuts, 5–10 minutes is ideal.

5. **Basting for Flavor**
   Basting meat during grilling adds layers of flavor and keeps it moist. Traditional Mexican BBQ often uses basting sauces with lime juice, beer, or even a splash of tequila. Apply basting sauces periodically throughout cooking to prevent drying and enhance flavor, particularly with chicken or pork.

6. **Experimenting with Wood Chips**
   Adding wood chips like mesquite, hickory, or applewood brings a smoky, authentic BBQ flavor. Soak the chips in water for about 30 minutes, then place them on the coals or in a smoker box. This is particularly effective for beef and pork dishes, adding depth to marinades and rubs.

Tips for Perfecting Mexican BBQ

1. **Fresh Ingredients Are Key**
   Fresh herbs, ripe limes, and authentic spices are essential for Mexican grilling. Using fresh ingredients not only enhances flavor but also helps maintain the authenticity of the dishes. Whenever possible, opt for fresh citrus juice, ripe tomatoes, and whole spices that you can grind yourself.

2. **Balancing Heat and Acidity**
   Mexican BBQ often balances heat from spices with acidity from lime or vinegar. This balance prevents dishes from becoming overly spicy and adds a refreshing element. To balance a spicy rub or marinade, add a

splash of lime juice or vinegar for brightness and flavor contrast.

3. **Resting and Carving Meat**
   After grilling, let meat rest and then slice against the grain, especially for cuts like skirt steak or flank steak. This method preserves tenderness and makes each bite more enjoyable, as slicing against the grain reduces chewiness.

4. **Garnishes to Enhance Flavor**
   Mexican BBQ dishes often benefit from fresh garnishes like chopped cilantro, diced onion, or crumbled cotija cheese. These garnishes add a final layer of flavor and texture, making each dish vibrant and visually appealing.

5. **Creating Versatile Salsas and Sides**
   Salsas, guacamole, and grilled vegetables are versatile sides that can complement almost any main dish. Prepare salsas ahead to allow flavors to meld, and experiment with grilled fruits or charred veggies like poblano peppers to add smokiness.

Made in the USA
Coppell, TX
28 January 2025